S.I.S.,

SPIRITUALLY INSPIRED SCRIPTS

VOLUME I

TAMI MAGBY

WESTBOW
P R E S S®
A DIVISION OF THOMAS NELSON
& ZONDERVAN

WestBow Press books may be ordered through booksellers or by contacting:

WestBow Press
A Division of Thomas Nelson & Zondervan
1663 Liberty Drive
Bloomington, IN 47403
www.westbowpress.com
844-714-3454

Scripture quotations are taken from the Holy Bible, New International Version®, NIV®.
Copyright © 1973, 1978, 1984 by Biblica, Inc.™
Used by permission of Zondervan. All rights reserved worldwide.

ISBN: 978-1-6642-9362-5 (sc)
ISBN: 978-1-6642-9361-8 (e)

Library of Congress Control Number: 2023905743

Print information available on the last page.

WestBow Press rev. date: 04/10/2023

Contents

Preface

A journey through life takes turns that leave one with lasting memories one may or may not be willing to share, especially not in depth, until the journey brings one to a place of unrelenting torment, forcing one to face the haunting fears that seem unwilling to decrease in impact. After many times of doing this cyclical dance, I made up my mind to receive the liberty that has been purchased for me and begin to walk in complete victory. "Blinded by His Touch; Made to See by His" is a reflection of the progressive stages I went through in taking that which was internal and manifesting it outwardly. My having been touched inappropriately at a young age led to perplexing behavior for which I, in my state of immaturity, wasn't prepared. This glimpse into my journey shows that moving from sheer grit and excruciating pain to whimsical expression in order to cope and come to a place of acceptance is what carried me through the cycles of psychological torment. Going from fighting a dysfunctional, almost crippling emotional battle to seeing God's Word transform my mind, making it a light amid the darkness, made all the difference. Indeed, God's light invaded the darkest crevices within me. I had to face my own giant and sort through what having been touched inappropriately as a preteen had ignited within me, knowing the limited capacity I had to make sense of what had happened. The images of those older men who sought after the little girl I was, those men who stirred the flaming torch within me, which sparked me to seek answers in all the wrong places, misguided as I was by a warped sense of love, were revolting. What did those men think their touches would form inside me? Over the years I grappled with these questions and found some answers. Now I am comfortable enough in my own skin to be able to stand up and say, "I'm free. I overcame, and I am well. In Jesus's name."

Blinded by his Touch; Made to See by His

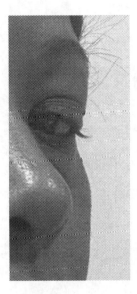

Whatever happened to the little girl who was violated at a young age? Whatever happened
to her?

Did anyone hear anything about how her life turned out?

As she retraces her own steps backward, then moves forward, going back and forth again and

again, she accounts for how those steps have landed her in this place today,

Now that His touch has made her *see*.

How could you leave me this way?

How could you not know that what you did would affect me negatively?

Did you not know it would be a lasting memory?

Did you know it would alter my view of how I see you?

Didn't you know it would leave a divide in my mind for years down the line?

How could you have left me with unanswered questions about why you did it?

Can you explain and help me to understand why you chose me as the one to invade?

Did you consider me lucky to have had your transgressions bestowed upon me?

There I was, dangling, loved by you as family but seduced by you when I was young and tender.

Help me understand; was I supposed to feel lucky? Or what about those who knew who you were and who knew you had trespassed against me but said absolutely nothing? How do I process this?

How do I consider them, then consider me? Is everyone in on it?

Long after you touched me, I've often wondered, did you forget you did it? Did your insides race with anxiety at the thought of ever seeing me again?

I wonder what you were thinking. How could you have left me like this? Did it happen to you too? Who made you believe that you could, or who built your confidence to enable you to, do such a thing? Who told you it was OK to treat me this way? From where did you get this assuredness? After all these years, do you ever wonder, *How could I have left her like that?*

Do you not know that at age forty-four I still feel your haunting shadow approach me, even in my dreams?

Do you not know the myriad escape routes I've chosen to flee from your hovering seduction?

Do you know how long your touch from yesteryear followed me into my new age?

Dust that's pale and lingers, that chokes and stifles.

Dust that clouds and invades.

The Dust Bowl ended faster than this horrific storm of oblivion that has planted itself securely within every part of me.

The period of the Dust Bowl, also known as the Dirty Thirties, passed by quicker than this love-hate relationship that has scorched me and warped my mind's eye, causing me to feel fear whenever I see any man approach.

How could you not know?

Am I mistaken in my assumption that we who suffered sexual abuse as children all take this kind of thing to heart after its introduction into our lives? Once innocent and delicate, we are now masked and saddled with residual memories of tenderness.

I was once blinded by his touch, but today I've been made to see by *His*.

I no longer feel the aching desire to call you and express how what you did affected me.

I've been sought after by another, whose touch has freed me to forgive you.

His touch has made me see light, love, splendor, glory, and beauty, none of which is tied to what you did.

There's no further explanation I desire from you.

I have Him. His touch did it all. I'm free!

I'm no longer blinded by your touch. No, now I see because of His!

The Ultimate Makeover

When you search through the layers,

When you search through life's intricacies,

What do you see?

With glistening eyes,

With an expectant heart,

With daring hands,

With unwavering knees,

And with plowed feet,

I see a man with astounding vision,

One willing to take what I have,

One willing to turn it into something greater.

A man who can see my new reality.

A man dutiful to aid in the manifestation

Of my becoming.

I see Tracy Thomas.

Thank you for making my dreams come true.

Petals like Wings

Just as the buds blossom, we ourselves unfold.

In many different ways, we reach upward and out.

O what a wonderful feeling it is to expand and know that from our Creator we have been given infinite possibilities.

In His hands He holds the power to do everything. He is all, and through Him we are on our way to full bloom; yet flourishing, we are blessed.

Continue to bud and blossom;

Your petals can take it.

Generations

I can only give you parts of who I am.

I must tell you, each part is pretty special.

The pretty special parts in me

Recognize the very special parts in you.

Let's stay together so that we make sure

Our extra special, extraordinary parts

Stay connected in part—closely connected, that is—forever.

The Heart of the Matter

The ray of light shines deep within me.

It shines bright enough for the world to see.

The flower flourishing in my heart,

The flower flourishing in my heart

Allows me to give the world something

So beautiful,

Something so rare—

My gift of love.

Our Covenant

As I began to tap into the potential for maximum love within me,

I began to pray for you.

I began to pray that the clouds would be your covering and

The angels your protection.

I began to pray that the beaming light from the sun draw us nearer.

I began to pray that the moon grace us with gentleness each time our thoughts lead us to hold

onto the love we've longed for all our lives.

Our maximum love potential, our desire to love, has guided us here

To stand before Almighty God,

To secure this union with our vows,

Forever being committed to reach maximum love together.

Here I stand submissive to our union.

To Us, For Us, About Us

I have waited all my life for this exact moment in time,

A time when my imagination of what love is

Connects with the reality of the love you and I share today.

We have found a love beyond measure in each other.

We create bliss that lingers within

To carry us into new seasons of love.

I'm still very much in love with you

Today, more than ever.

Here's to us!

Wait in Trust

As you walk your steps won't be hindered. As you run you will not stumble.
—Proverbs 4:12

No snare of the enemy can outwill the will of God.

Be mindful of who's in control and to whom to entrust all your

Situations and circumstances. You may not know the answers to

The questions of why, when, or how, but because you know Him,

Even as a shadow, an inkling, or a towering citadel, it's enough

To allow you to continue on in His peace until your prayers are answered.

Genetically Inclined

Although it may not have been spoken,

Although some measuring may say its weight is small,

I watched you through innocent lenses and imitated you.

I aped your gestures as I knew that some part of who you were was part of me too.

Don't take these things lightly, because

I will always reflect upon part of whom I am,

Retrospectively envisioning how I came to be me—

And in part it's because of you.

Being a part of you is a great force behind who I have become.

I'm proud to tell the world that you are my family.

Magnified

Take in my beauty

And float indeed.

Allow your heart to chortle.

Your eyes of love found my burning candle,

An infinite light for us to lie by.

For Our Fathers

Your strength is recognized by those who have had a glimpse into your life.

The strength of your hands that diligently work to make things happen for others,

To create ways for others,

Is never disregarded.

The look in your eyes as you venture off into the unknown,

Visualizing the greatness you'll take part in to make a world of difference,

Will never be forgotten.

Your heart that extends to those close and dear to you

As you speak encouraging words

Is always anticipated.

These are just a few of the things you are loved and cherished for,

And on this special day,

You are deserving of the highest recognition

For affecting the lives of those around you in a hearty way

With love.

I celebrate you, Dad.

For My Grandmother, Mother, Father, Aunts, and Uncles

Now unto him who is able to keep you from falling.

—Jude 1:24

There is something you need to know this day.

I could not let another day pass by without saying how special you are to me.

From you I have been given a glimpse of the strength that a wonderful man or woman should exhibit and extend to those around them.

Because of your strength, because of your willingness to go through the trials of life and remain firm in your stance to achieve all that is due to you, because of your unselfish deeds, because you extended your love, opening your arms to give hugs, because you continued to uphold the image of a warrior—all these things contribute to my having become who I am today and who I aspire to be going forward. At times when I want to give in to the woes of life, I see an image of your strength and how you pressed forward. When I wanted to settle for less, I saw how you continued through your pains and struggles to present your best to me. For this, I thank you.

In Your Honor, Mrs. J

And he opened their understanding that they might comprehend.
—Luke 24:5

Your persistence hasn't gone unnoticed.

What you've taught me will soon be revealed,

The inner workings of building skills and enhancing minds,

To be on display for a grander stand in your honor

As you work to make sure I stand—

Stand more equipped with knowledge,

Stand in confidence to close the gaps unscaled,

And stand with new direction to make sure I, among other things, am healed,

Healed from the distress of not having enough

When more is deemed necessary,

Healed to carry forth new hope in becoming yet more,

Defined within.

Now I stand

And

I'm healed.

Now my grander stand in your honor is here.

Your persistence hasn't gone unnoticed.

What you've taught me is now on display

In part, but not wholly revealed.

I stand; I am healed,

And I continue to hope

As I become yet more,

Defined within.

I'm able to take this grander stand in part because of what you've taught,

The inner workings of building skills and enhancing minds.

This grander stand is in your honor.

Hearts Intertwined on Valentine's Day

The branch of the Lord shall be beautiful and glorious.

—Isaiah 4:2

My heart has grown to love you more since our day of bliss,

Since our day of vowing to hold onto each other's hearts with tenderness,

Since we stood in the presence of our heavenly Father and declared our love to the world.

This day I pronounce as ours, a day to love each other more, a day to honor our unconditional

union, never forgetting that

We are propped up by grace

In the good times

Or that sometimes grace steps in to deliver a circumstance

Not so pleasing, but altogether welcome

Because we know it's required for deeper love.

This Love Day. I pronounce my love to you again,

Louder, deeper, and with immense passion,

Proclaiming, "I'm honored to be your missus."

Tracy's Dream

Blessed is the man who is steadfast under trial and perseveres when tempted.
—James 1:12

As the passing days gapingly move beyond,

Her mind's eye opens more readily to

The possibilities of making her dreams a reality

With toiling hands doing the mending.

Her heart is elated by each task

That draws her nearer to her dreams

With the wrenching challenges grasping at her heels.

Her eyes are propped open until

Each task's completion.

Once again her heart is elated,

Now even more

By each task that draws her dream nearer.

With every scar inflicted by voices of defiance,

With calamities echoing in her ear,

She realizes these are but glimpses of what was.

Now each scar is healed,

A mere reflection of all that's behind her.

Again and again

Closer, her heart's bliss rings,

Quenching the thirst

That once only a dream could fulfill.

Now reality has set in.

This day, Tracy's dream is a reality.

This marks just the beginning of many

Days and nights to come

When her heart is elated more and more

By each task

Until each of her dreams

Becomes a reality.

A Little Is a Lot

Caring is wonderful;

However, showing you care

By sharing is uplifting.

Thanks for the lift you gave me.

I sure needed it!

Only You

When I spoke, "Not my will, but Your will, O God,"

Prayers I have prayed began to float in the atmosphere, and an

Illuminating light began to hit them.

The prayers began to dance about to a sweet melody.

Father, only You are able to bring words to life.

As the course of my life takes a new direction,

I thank You for the beautiful gift of spiritual vision.

Reflections

At that moment, I knew

I was capturing a glimpse

Of perfection in my life.

A memory made

Is a memory gained.

Times spent capturing moments with you

Will be well spent forever.

In Honor of You, William Edward Collins III

Rejoice in that day. Leap for Joy. For great is your reward in heaven.

—Luke 6:23

William, as you reach maturity,

As you are presented to the world as a responsible young man,

I'd like to personally applaud you!

First, I applaud you for recognizing the importance of responsibility

To yourself.

At the end of each day, *you* must be *proud* of *you*.

Second, I applaud you for your hopeful outlook on what's in store for you.

You have been created in the image of our Father in heaven.

You are well equipped to reach any level of success

In spite of any internal conflict or

External circumstance.

Your good success is important to God.

I recognize you today for your awakening moment,

When making your mark on the world became most important to you.

I'm proud of you, Son!

A Mother's Love for Her Son

A mother should teach her son in the way he

Should go, according to God's Word, for then he will never depart from it.

I shall teach you to love yourself without compromise

While loving others just the same.

I shall teach you to pray and know you can never go

So far that God won't be able to find you or

Answer you

No matter when you call upon Him.

I shall teach you how to live with

Dignity,

Integrity,

Confidence,

And boldness,

And with great expectations of success in every area

Of your life.

Because I love you, I must teach you. I must demonstrate these things, along with many others, so that you too can pass on such love and more.

Lord, give me wisdom. Teach me to be the mother he needs at every stage of his life.

Who Is He?

The words leaped from the pages of the Holy Book, an astonishing account of great men and women of God and of how they rested in their anointing power straight from heaven above, captivating the crowds with the *dunamis* power forging through the atmosphere to pierce every unclean thing so as to make the environment right for the Spirit of God to dwell.

Here I stand in awe of an experience that was just like that,

A view spectacular, with all the glitz and glamour imaginable, but not anything the natural eyes can behold. I speak of glory falling like drops of radiant light, drops that flow from heaven like a musical melody. Before the glory lands on flesh, the individual, in anticipation, receives the power, welcoming it with open arms and joy, a great release of something unimaginable, ignited by God but ushered in by a mighty man of God.

Who Is He?

He's a man who worships unceasingly, a man who runs to the Master for the wisdom to lead people in need. He runs to the Master to seek counsel. He runs to the Master for approval. He runs to the Master to rejoice. He runs to the Master to exalt His holy name, causing it to reverberate throughout the earth in appreciation for the work done to change his life eternal.

Who Is He?

The anointed man of God.

Coming to Terms

I've dealt with it within myself:

The bliss of our kisses,

The exuberance of our chemistry.

I've dealt with the mysteries of our time apart,

The vulnerable side of me conspiring against my worth as a woman,

Battling with the spirit of rejection that comes to my mind and to my heart.

I take a closer look to determine how I feel about rejection

And, if I have been rejected, how I internalize the experience.

I've resolved that I am vulnerable but no less worthy of love.

I've resolved that I love to love and that I love the growth potential surrounding love.

I've resolved that I'm at peace with analyzing each of these things from zero to one hundred.

I've resolved that after undergoing this scrutiny-heavy yet liberating experience, I am made from love. And I richly embrace loving myself more as I undergo each encounter that prompts the analysis leading to revelation.

I've resolved that the risk I'd have to take while seeking out love, while exercising my heart in exploration of love's reward, is something I'd accept, sometimes daily, always in moderation, sometimes as needed. It just depends on, whether consistently or intermittently, I have faith in divine love, ordained and sent to me by the One who composed my infinitely intricate being. I have taken this to the Potter, for I am the clay which He alone composed. And He is the One who has given me rest in all these things. So I go, refreshed again to continue on.

Family Proclamation 1

God of all consolation, I proclaim Your Word over my family line, the Magby House.
Every seed I'm connected to by blood and spirit I pronounce life over. I speak order, peace,
wholeness, divine health, the mind of Christ, prosperity, true riches, courage, exceeding faith,
boldness, integrity, liberty, honor, and hearts within all of us that thirst after You.

In the matchless name of Jesus, I declare the devil, his workers, and all their works null and
void. Lord, with Your consuming fire all his dealings concerning this family line are destroyed.
I proclaim that Your reigning, ruling power leads us into divine protection, for the Trinity is
our Doorkeeper and Gatekeeper. Lamb of God, send forth Your resurrecting power through
this generational line and down through ages to heal all wounds, mend every tear, and cover
every scar. Breath of Life, breathe a refreshing breath up through our generational line, where
the devil has come in to steal, kill, and destroy. Holy Spirit of promise, refresh us, restore us,

and propel us to operate in the fullness in which God has created us to function, as He had in mind from the very beginning, in every area of our lives. Make us operate in "now faith" so we may experience the dimension where "eyes have not seen, ears have not heard, and neither has it entered the hearts of men, the things that God has in store for us" (1 Corinthians 2:9). Make our lives to be in direct unison with the will of God because we honor what Jesus did on the cross and so our lives won't be lived in vain. We honor You, our Diadem of Beauty, and count these things done in the matchless name of Jesus Christ of Nazareth. Amen, family.

Family Proclamation II: The Magby Men

I extend my love to each of you on this day set aside just for you.

My prayer has been focused on the supernatural power of God, hoping it would begin flowing like never before throughout the Magby line. You all make up the foundation of this family, so I especially ask God to move in a mighty way to reposition each of you into your rightful places. May your hearts be open to receive what God has in store for our entire family, beginning with you.

I declare that every generational curse, every binding and hindering thing that has lingered within the Magby line, be broken, that the right hand of God in His glory disperse power up through our family line. From this day forward, may each of you operate with a greater level of faith. "Faith is the substance of things hoped for and the evidence of things not seen" (Hebrews 11:1). Now is a critical time for us to consistently seek God for each one of our family members to be saved, liberated, and set free. We must begin to live life more abundantly. Later for merely surviving. Let us each embrace the most that heaven has to offer us spiritually, emotionally, physically, and financially. With the strength that each of you bring to this family, every single prayer that we stand on corporately will be heard by God. By faith, I believe He is waiting on us to ask, and He will answer. I ask each of you to use your strength to work things out so that our entire line will rise up and become everything we are supposed to be. I have drawn my strength, my motivation, and my intelligence from each of you. I love you all dearly and commend you on your willingness to keep on keeping on. The happiest of Father's Days to each of you!

Family Proclamation III: Christmastime

In celebration of Jesus Christ, let us all welcome Him, in whose honor we celebrate this day and this season. Jesus, we welcome Your presence in this place. Happy birthday to You. We love You.

To our Father in heaven, the Father of Abraham, Isaac, and Jacob, from whom all blessings flow; as it was with them, so it is with us. With that being said, let us all receive in our hearts the plan He has spoken over us, a plan of greatness, wholeness, prosperity, authority, divine health, peace, and the unspeakable joy that only He can give.

To the head of the family, Sarah Magby, I say, thank you. Thank you for standing for each of us and for believing way down in your spirit when everything appeared to be against us. As we have all come a mighty long way, starting in our minds, I declare by the authority of Jesus Christ working in me that we no longer conform to those binding and hindering things of old. The curse is broken. I declare that we stand up by faith with submissive hearts to do what is pleasing to God. He created us; therefore, everything we need to walk though this world, He has already ordained. By faith I call forth strength, obedience, courage, and wisdom to enable us to fall into line with God's plan, relinquishing our desire to do it our way. God has called each of us to help heal one another, to restore each other, and to build each other up. Let these prayers be carried forth so they will manifest. May the scars and bruises on our hearts be mended this day. May we encounter the holy Trinity (the Father, the Son, and the Holy Spirit) like never before.

Again, I declare that our family line is blessed. Let's all say it: the Magby line is blessed, healed, delivered, and set free. As the Word of God says, "Our boundary lines have landed in pleasant places" (Psalm 16:6). Be it unto each of us, O God, that we receive what is stirring within us, seeds You planted even before the foundation of the world. We receive Your promises of truth this day, in Jesus's name, amen.

No Longer in Rotation

No need to look, no need to search, no need to wonder.

No need to look, no need to search, no need to wonder.

I just can't go on with the inconsistencies that go along

With a relationship I just can't depend on.

I'll never give into it.

I'd rather be here loving you, boy,

Holding onto you.

I just want to be with you. I wanna be near, so

No need to look, no need to search, no need to wonder.

No need to look, no need to search, no need to wonder.

Becoming

When I look up into the sky,

I can't imagine why,

Can't imagine why,

We hurt each other and do harm to each other.

When I look up into the sky,

I can't imagine why,

Can't imagine why, we do what we do.

The power we hold, we must not know.

I ask, "Why do we doubt it?"

We couldn't do anything without it.

When I look up into the sky,

I can't imagine why,

Can't imagine why,

We continue to

Go on and do wrong.

The gifts we bring to a place we call our own.

We must change to continue on.

I don't really want to live like this.

I don't really want to live like this.

No Restraints

To embrace you on a day

I've often longed for.

I'm so glad to have you.

I'm so glad I found you and your love. You make me very happy.

All day long, you're on my mind. I just can't stop thinking about you.

Baby, I love the way you love me so between the sheets.

How could I, how could I ever, let you go?

You know we belong together.

And when you take my hand and lead me into a place,

Heaven only knows.

'Cause you're my man. You know you know. The way you make me feel,

Baby-aby-aby, ah, aw, ooh, ooh.

I need you. Right here. Right now. Right here. Right now.

Miracles from On High

A united stand we take in terms of the way we want our lives to be.

Trendsetters,

Hype pushers,

Love givers.

Creations of strength and might, we are.

We have visions and see that we are royalty.

Regal we are, treading away from the past, losing it in the dust.

The trenches make way for our new harvest, for all of us, not just one.

This is our flesh in action trying to catch up to the spirit.

Press

Opt not to be tired

But to be ready.

Explore every possibility there is to explore.

Understand that each opportunity plays a role.

Keep on movin'.

Don't stop.

Little Girl

Mom, you were the first to tell me to always hold my head up

And to understand why I should.

You were the first to tell me life is full of ups and downs

But that I could make it through them all.

You have been my personal cheerleader many times when I couldn't see clearly. You always said, "It will be all right."

Mom, I'm so proud that you have been so many things to me over the years. I'm so proud you were chosen to be my mom. Only you could have loved me, nurtured me, and blessed my life the way you have. I love you, Mom, and I celebrate this day honoring you.

Happy Mother's Day!

Letter to My Son

With maturity, you must learn that no personality conflict should negatively affect your inner drive. It should never overwhelm you. Impeding situations should make you dig more deeply within to find a way to rise above it all.

You must, without a doubt, become a better learner of life's lessons. Then you must be a doer of what you've learned, being wiser, using choice words with a winning attitude. You must not let anything stand in your way. Go around any obstacle. Find the right way to rise above.

Peace We Must Have

I haven't been where I'm going, but I'm going there.

I didn't know I could get here, but I did get here.

So, if I'm sure to go forward,

I can't help but make the trip a good one.

The steps I must climb,

The journey I must see through.

The light I see on the other side

Somehow moves me closer to you,

Even when the distance seems far.

I can't help but want to be where you are.

No matter how hard it gets,

I still won't quite be there until I feel Your Spirit deeply rooted in me,

till the winds, the storms, and the seas stop, causing me to realize,

This road I'm traveling is solely for me. Nothing can stop me.

The Country

The heart, so true, sometimes blue.

The beat so rhythmic, setting the pace to uplift.

The eyes so open to see the light, all colors, along with laughter and enjoyment.

To be alone and running through a field of beauty,

One filled with lilies, dandelions, and orchids,

The scent of the wild greenery all around,

With me saying, *I'm free to enjoy all this. All things, they are mine.*

I take great delight in them. I say, "Thank You," as I fall on my back,

Looking up at the sky so blue, with the puffiness of the clouds softening

The picture my mind's eye is closing in on. Such a joy to be out in nature:

The trees hovering over me. The shade they bring. The breeze I feel. The love I hold.

Overpowering, it is. Overwhelming for sure. I realize it is real. no denial permitted.

Accept it, enjoy it, be of it: it's in me.

Within Arm's Reach

Have you ever looked into the eyes of a gentleman and just knew his touch would be tender?

Awaiting our next encounter to confirm I will eventually surrender. I find myself getting lost in your soulfulness, your masculinity warms me.

Surrounded by a feeling so sincere, I always want to have you near, right next to me.

I'm looking forward to the next time when our hearts are able to flow to a tune so smooth with a vibe so strong, me just knowing nothing can go wrong;

I give a subtle hint to him saying, stay with me, baby, 'cause you don't know what you're in for. You have never experienced a love so true. The love I've got, you can't withstand, so give in to me now.

If not now, eventually you will. Time will cause you to give in willingly, then surrender to love in unison with me. My love for you is true.

Let Me Be Clear

If I can't trust you

If I can't respect you

Love is just a fairytale

Printed in the United States
by Baker & Taylor Publisher Services